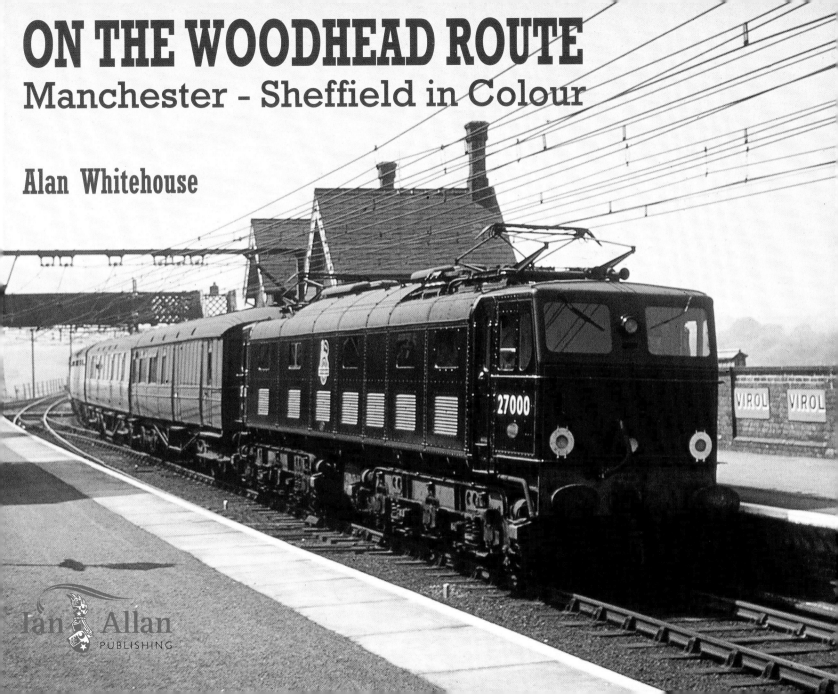

ON THE WOODHEAD ROUTE
Manchester - Sheffield in Colour

Alan Whitehouse

Ian Allan
PUBLISHING

Introduction

Front cover: The late 1960s brought a splendid mix of colours to the railway scene, summed up here by No E26050 *Stentor* in Rail blue with early yellow warning panel, red buffer-beam and 'lion' totem! The train is almost equally colourful — a mix of the emergent blue and grey, the redundant maroon, and a renegade Southern Region green vehicle. *Stentor* is working one of the hourly expresses to Sheffield, and is pictured near Thurgoland in December 1969. *Peter Hughes / Colour-Rail DE544*

Back cover: By 1970 the Woodhead route had become a rather basic railway, passenger trains having ceased and freight traffic being in decline. Here No E26009 heads west with a classic Woodhead load of unfitted coal. *Gavin Morrison*

Title page: Dinting station sat across a triangular junction giving access to the short Glossop branch from both east and west. Roaring through on the main line to Sheffield is 'EM2' No 27000, soon to be named *Electra*, in the original black, red-lined livery worn by all the electric fleet. The coaching stock appears to be Gresley-designed and the second vehicle, at least, is wearing the delightful 1950s 'blood and custard' colour scheme. *The late W. Oliver / Colour-Rail DE1126*

First published 2001

ISBN 0 7110 2784 6

© Alan Whitehouse 2001

Published by Ian Allan Publishing

an imprint of Ian Allan Publishing Ltd, Terminal House, Shepperton, Surrey TW17 8AS.
Printed by Ian Allan Printing Ltd, Hersham, Surrey KT12 4RG.

Code: 0102/B1

It is difficult to say exactly when the idea of electrifying the railway over Woodhead was born. As early as 1913, C. W. Neele, the Great Central Railway's Electrical Engineer, believed electrification of at least the Wath–Penistone section was the only answer to seemingly endless growth in coal traffic and the congestion it was creating.

Neele had just seen new electric locomotives for the Butte, Anaconda & Pacific Railroad whilst on a visit to the United States. The BA&P locomotivess were used in pairs, ferrying copper ore from mine to smelter. His idea was taken no further, but turned out to be almost prophetic. At about the same time, the Newport–Shildon line was demonstrating that main-line electrification was a serious possibility.

A second scheme, this time to electrify the whole Woodhead route, was proposed in 1926, but made little headway. Finally, in 1935, with the promise of Government money, the LNER began work on a major electrification project between Manchester and Sheffield and the branch from Penistone to Wath.

A locomotive was designed — and a start made on building it — and gantries were erected before war put the project on ice. The first locomotive, numbered 6701, was completed and tested, then stored.

Postwar, the Woodhead project was again revived, this time in a bigger and better form than ever. A total of 85 locomotives was planned, a new tunnel was to be driven through the hills at Woodhead at a cost of £3 million, and overhead wiring would reach around Manchester to Central station in addition to London Road (later renamed Piccadilly). There was even talk of extending the electrification beyond Sheffield, to Whitemoor Yard in the east, or down the Great Central main line to Marylebone.

Economic facts of life quickly got in the way, and electrification into Manchester Central was dropped, an order for 27 express locomotives was cut to just seven, and all talk of extensions was quietly dropped.

A revised version of the original LNER locomotive was adopted, and a class of 57 (instead of the 69 originally envisaged) was built at Gorton Works. They were known as 'EM1s' (Electric Mixed-traffic Type 1) and were followed by the seven 'EM2s'. The final one of these, No 27006, became the last locomotive to be built at Gorton. Additionally, a small fleet of three-car multiple-units was built to handle suburban trains between Manchester, Hadfield and Glossop.

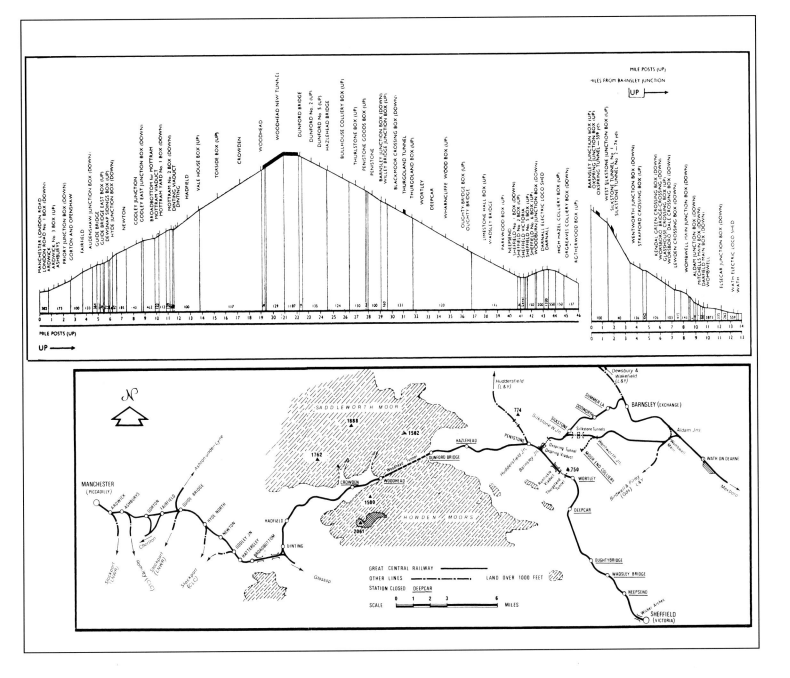

MILE POSTS (UP)

MILES FROM BARNSLEY JUNCTION

UP →

MILE POSTS (UP)

UP →

The locomotives were innovative, taking advantage of the long gradients on either side of the Pennines to use regenerative braking. This effectively transforms the locomotive into a generator, feeding current back into the overhead line rather than drawing it out. This action creates resistance, and this is used to brake the train, both saving wear on conventional brakes and ending the need to stop and pin down wagon brakes on unfitted trains.

On the Worsborough branch regenerative braking also allowed banking engines to perform useful work in both directions; instead of immediately heading back down the gradient after banking a train to the top, the locomotives were stabled, waiting for a train to go down. Coupled on the front, the banker and train engine were able to 'regen' down the bank, both braking their own train and generating power for those climbing the incline.

The first stage of the system became operational on 4 February 1952, when electric traction took over between Wath Yard and Dunford Bridge via the Worsborough branch. Phase Two — Dunford Bridge to Manchester — went live in 1954, with the first train through the new Woodhead Tunnel. In 1955 a full changeover was effected and the Woodhead route became, in the words of a commemorative poster produced at the time, 'Britain's First All-Electric Main Line'.

In the early years traffic was heavy, and the new electrics found plenty of work. But, from the start, the Woodhead scheme was destined to be a one-off — an island of non-standard equipment. Technology had moved on, and all future railway electrification would be to the new 25kV AC standard.

By the late 1960s British Rail had announced its new trans-Pennine strategy: Woodhead would become a freight-only route, able to function more effectively if the freights did not have to be constantly looped out of the way of fast passenger trains. Thus the final regular passenger service ran on 5 January 1970.

Alongside this, there had been another, more positive development. As originally built, the 'EM1s' had neither air braking (except for a straight air brake on the locomotive) nor multiple-unit control. A batch of 21 was converted between 1968 and 1970, later followed by another nine. They were intended to operate in pairs (shades of the old BA&P Railroad), working block trains of coal from pit to power station, the new 'merry-go-round'(MGR) system. It worked well, and the 'EM1s', reclassified as Class 76 under the new BR numbering scheme, came to be seen as competent and reliable, taking 1,400-ton trains over the difficult Worsborough and Woodhead road with few problems.

Other traffic, however, was fast disappearing as the rules governing freight-train subsidies changed and road competition increased. By the late 1970s it was becoming clear that, contrary to its statements about needing a freight route across the Pennines, British Rail now saw little future at all for the Woodhead line.

The end finally came on 17 July 1981, after a seven-week reprieve for additional talks with the trades unions. Shortly after midday, a pair of Class 76s made their way along the Worsborough branch and it closed for ever. The final MGR coal working left Barnsley Junction late the same evening, and in the early hours of the morning, the last train of all — a Speedlink working from Harwich to Liverpool — passed through the 'new' Woodhead Tunnel and the main line also closed.

At the insistence of the unions, one line was left in place, but reopening was never a serious possibility, and the final rails were lifted some three years later, leaving suburban services from Manchester to Hadfield, a freight branch from Sheffield to Deepcar, and a diverted Huddersfield–Penistone–Sheffield passenger service running via Barnsley.

Was there any alternative to closure? Sadly, probably not. Coal was the main reason for building the Woodhead line in the first place, and the only reason for building the Worsborough branch and the yard at Wath. If Woodhead had survived in 1981, it would surely have gone in the rundown of the mining industry that followed the strike of 1984/5.

Like the Newport–Shildon scheme which preceded it, Woodhead fell victim to changed traffic patterns, but also a change in technology. It was a curious end for what, only 29 years before, had been a showpiece.

Alan Whitehouse
December 2000

Right: Red-letter day: the Manchester–Sheffield–Wath electrified lines officially opened for business in June 1954, although the first revenue-earning trains ran in 1952 between Wath and Dunford Bridge. Here Class EM1 No 26020 performs the opening ceremony at the new Woodhead station. It is about the enter the newly-bored Woodhead Tunnel, inaugurating 'Britain's First All-Electric Main Line'.
K. Oldham / Colour-Rail DE1203

The new system began at the buffers of Manchester's newly-renamed Piccadilly station, and here No E26053 *Perseus* stands at the head of a Sheffield express in August 1968. The locomotive's recently-applied coat of Rail blue with arrows symbol is already grimed with road dust.
Gavin Morrison

In the same year, No E26054 *Pluto* reverses slowly into Platform 1 to collect an express service to Sheffield. In contrast to *Perseus*, this locomotive is still in Brunswick green with small yellow warning panel. The service has been running barely 13 years, but already there is talk of the passenger trains being axed and when it finally is, *Pluto* will achieve an unwelcome fame by working one of the last regular passenger service over Woodhead on 5 January 1970. *T. J. Edgington / Colour-Rail DE1349*

Below: Green began to take over from black as 'EM1' livery from the late 1950s, and in 1960 No 26035 got the full treatment in Gorton Works. It is seen here looking splendid in lined green with cream roof. The roofs of Woodhead-line electrics were always painted a light shade of cream or primrose, even when corporate blue livery was introduced. Even after the end of steam, the roofs quickly became dirty and after a few months gave the appearance of a grey roof with light weathering. No 26035 was scrapped in 1970, and its number taken by 76018 after conversion to a multiple-unit-fitted locomotive for a new role of hauling heavy merry-go-round coal trains. *T. B. Owen / Colour-Rail DE542*

Right: Under the original plans, three maintenance depots were planned for the MSW system, but Reddish, just around the corner from Gorton, was chosen to maintain the whole fleet. Less than two months before the Woodhead route closed, No 76 038 and another unidentified member of the class receive attention alongside Class 40 diesels. *Tony Miles*

Left: Even after the system closed and the '76s' were officially withdrawn, two of them, Nos 76 003 (vacuum-only) and 76 015 (air-fitted), were still working as depot shunters. No 76 015 is pictured standing outside the depot building. *Tony Miles*

Above: Guide Bridge was the first major stop after Manchester. Class EM2 No E27000 *Electra* has charge of a Sheffield-bound express in May 1967. A little over a year later, the locomotive would be withdrawn and later sold to Netherlands Railways, where it lasted in service until 1986. Only seven 'EM2s' were built and, although written evidence is lacking, it seems likely that they were intended as a 'pre-series' build to test the design of a 90mph electric locomotive, possibly for use on the GC main line to Marylebone. Whatever the reason, a 90mph locomotive on a route with a 65mph line speed made little sense. An 'EM1', No E26019, rolls light-engine into the down platform. *B. Magilton / Colour-Rail DE713*

Left: Starting in the late 1960s, batches of the 'EM1' locomotives were modified to operate in multiple under the control of one driver, and were fitted with air brakes. Looking east from Guide Bridge, two of the first batch, Nos 76 027 and 76 026, roll into Guide Bridge with a rake of 21-ton hoppers in early 1979. *Gavin Morrison*

Right: Just as the Woodhead line declined in importance, so did Guide Bridge. By the late 1970s, the expresses had gone and the station was served by the fleet of eight three-car electric multiple-units built for suburban traffic between Manchester, Hadfield and Glossop. Guide Bridge today is even more a shadow of its former self: the station buildings in the background have been demolished and used to fill the well between the two platforms seen here. Trains now use the remaining two platform faces at what has become a depressing, inner-city unstaffed halt. *Neil Moxham*

Left: In the happier days of September 1966, the pioneer electric, No E26000 *Tommy*, is seen just off the platform ends. Green livery and small yellow warning panels make this a classic 'sixties view. The locomotive had a smaller cab than the production version, and the lack of quarterlight and opening side window are evident. The changes were made when engine crews complained of the lack of visibility. The windscreens were also enlarged, the drivers' side being equipped with an electric screen heater — long before the idea was taken up by car manufacturers!
B. Magilton / Colour-Rail DE716

Left: Godley Junction was a major exchange point for traffic on and off the Manchester–Sheffield–Wath system, and many trains changed traction here. Class 76s Nos 76 023 and 76 022, however, are rattling straight through with a trainload of 'HEA' coal hoppers six weeks before closure, in June 1981. *Ken Braithwaite*

Below: During the conversion to electrification, Hattersley Tunnel was excavated to form a cutting instead. An unidentified Class 76 heads an eastbound train of unbraked 16-ton coal empties through the cutting in February 1970. The locomotive sports an 'E'-prefix number and a 'ferret and dartboard' logo. *David Birch*

Inset: 'EM2' No 27005 with a Sheffield-bound express near Mottram in 1956. The black livery, bold original British Railways logo and polished metalwork arguably suited the Woodhead-line locomotives better than anything subsequently applied. No 27005 was later named *Minerva*. *The late W. Oliver / Colour-Rail DE538*

Left: Dinting Viaduct was strengthened with additional piers well before the electrification project began. No 76 046, its *Archimedes* nameplates long since removed, crosses with an eastbound haul of coal empties in December 1976. *Les Nixon*

Below: Dinting had a small shed in steam days, and electric locomotives often used the shed yard. But appearances are deceptive. This view dates from June 1981, not the 1950s. No 26020 had been restored to original condition three years before as part of the National Collection. It took part in the 150th anniversary celebrations of the Liverpool & Manchester Railway in 1980, and is seen here after arriving at the Dinting Railway Centre — housed in the former shed — where it remained for several years. No 26020 is now in the National Railway Museum at York. *Ken Braithwaite*

Above: A Manchester–Hadfield–Glossop unit stands in one of the sharply-curved platforms at Dinting that give access to the Glossop branch, in the summer of 1977. When the new electric suburban service was launched in 1954, patronage went up by an astonishing 140%. *Alan Whitehouse*

Right: One of the eight units built for the service has just left Dinting and is passing over the Glossop end of the triangular junction. In this 1981 view, the track has been singled and the signalbox demolished. *R. T. Nunn*

Left: Glossop station itself was always a fairly modest affair, with one main platform face. By the time this picture was taken in November 1979, that is all that was left in use, served by a single line. The electric suburban units had by now been classified '506', and were to last another three years after the main line had been closed and the 'EM1' fleet withdrawn. They were finally axed in December 1984 when the lines to Glossop and Hadfield were re-electrified using the 25kV AC system — something that BR insisted was impractical and too expensive for the main line over Woodhead. *Les Nixon*

Below: Hadfield station was terminus for the Manchester suburban service and the Class 506 units rarely ran beyond this point. When the Manchester–Sheffield passenger service was up for closure, there was a proposal to extend the Hadfield service to Penistone — just 15 miles away — to connect with the Huddersfield–Sheffield service, but a combination of factors (including the fact that the Class 506s had gearing that was too low to cope with the climb to Woodhead without overheating) put paid to the idea. *Alan Whitehouse*

It is easy to forget that the 'EM1' and 'EM2' electrics worked alongside steam for many years — they were built five years before the first production diesels appeared. Here, No 26043 pilots an ex-ROD 'O4' 2-8-0. The 'EM1s' displaced the 'O4s', which had been the mainstay of the Woodhead line since before World War 1. The picture was taken at Torside crossing in June 1954, just before full electric services began. *K. Oldham / Colour-Rail DE1204*

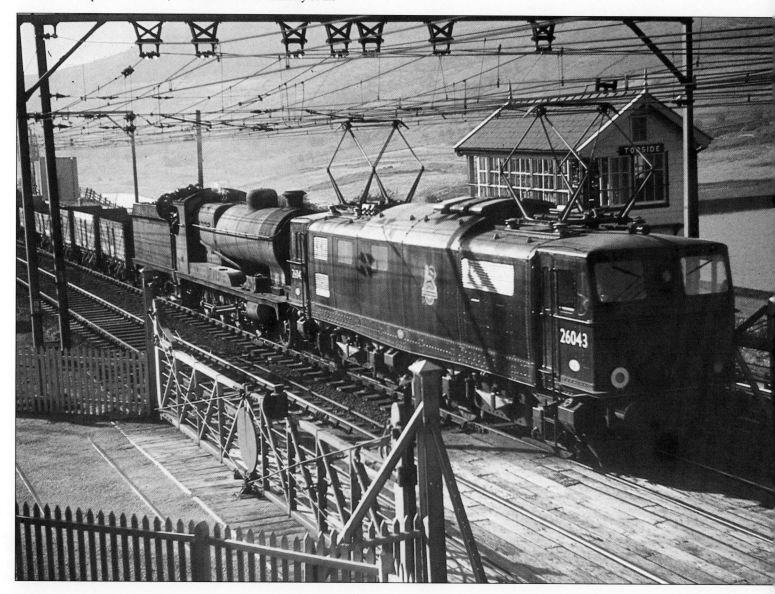

Like certain steam locomotives before them, the new 'EM1s' were quickly found to be capable of pulling rather more than they could stop in a hurry. Before the lesson was learned, and maximum train weights reduced, there were several near misses at Torside, where a down loop on a long downhill gradient ended a few yards short of the crossing. Even regenerative braking power was not enough to prevent No 26019 coming to grief in 1954, only a short time after this section was opened to electric traction. Two years later No 26004 repeated the trick, whilst 12 months after that No 26017 demolished part of the crossing gates. *The late W. Oliver / Colour-Rail DE539*

Above: One of No 76 046's more unusual tasks was to work a charter special composed of preserved Great Western Railway coaching stock over the line in May 1976. The ensemble, corporate Rail blue contrasting vividly with chocolate and cream, is seen at Torside crossing. *Les Nixon*

Right: Just five months to go before closure, but MU locomotives Nos 76 006 and 76 024 look well cared for — shiny even — as they head a westbound haul of power-station coal through Longdendale, near Crowden, in February 1981. *Les Nixon*

Duties for vacuum-only single locomotives were fast disappearing when this picture was taken in April 1980, but No 76 046 finds useful work hauling a string of empty 21-ton hoppers back to Orgreave, near Rotherwood Exchange sidings. This locomotive, formerly *Archimedes*, was one of 14 'EM1s' given train heating boilers to allow them to deputise for the 'EM2' class; when passenger services ceased, the boilers were gradually removed. The picture was taken a short distance east of Crowden station. *Les Nixon*

From almost the same spot, a view of Nos 76 029 and 76 030 with a full MGR train heading west. The '76s' will take the train as far as Mottram, where the former marshalling yard has by now been reduced to a small fan of exchange sidings for the purpose of changing traction, almost invariably to a Class 47 diesel. *Les Nixon*

Above: Sheep hurriedly vacate the up main as a pair of air-fitted '76s', Nos 76 025 and 76 027, tackle the climb to Woodhead with a BOC block tank train for Broughton Lane, Sheffield. The air-braking and multiple-unit equipment was fitted to Class 76s primarily for MGR coal working, but turned the electrics into versatile workhorses. *Ken Braithwaite*

Right: It was uncommon to see a single MU-fitted locomotive on an MGR or other 'double-load' working: No 76 030, seen here in July 1980, is perfectly capable of tackling the final stages of the ascent to Woodhead with 30 MGR empties in tow, but will be unable to make the return trip with a loaded MGR train unassisted. *M. M. Hughes*

Left: Nos 76 021 and 76 015 emerge from the western portal of the new Woodhead Tunnel in May 1981 with the inevitable set of loaded MGR wagons in tow. Typically, for the months leading up to closure, the lead locomotive has one marker light out. By this time, any repair work seemed beside the point. *Les Nixon*

Below: Woodhead winter: a pair of '76s' trailing steel flats encounter a snowy landscape as they leave the tunnel. This is the end of April 1981, and the snowfall makes the stories of horrific Pennine winters perfectly believable. Almost identical stations were built at each tunnel mouth. The architecture was modern, the material traditional stone. Both included large and well-heated signalboxes, but both this station and Dunford Bridge at the other end of the tunnel saw little use, and closed well before the final demise of the passenger service. *Ken Braithwaite*

Left: An unidentified pair of MU-fitted '76s', this time with a load of hoppers, approach Woodhead on a dreary day in 1978. *Alan Whitehouse*

Below: It will have been a long haul from Sheffield for a solo Class 76 — the BOC tank train it is hauling normally required the services of a pair of engines — but the train is now just a few hundred yards from the eastern portal of the tunnel at Dunford Bridge. A short way into the tunnel, and the gradient changes abruptly from a climb to the long descent to Manchester. *Ken Braithwaite*

Another Dunford Bridge view, this time dating from 1970, of 'celebrity' locomotive No 76 020, by now in Rail blue, but still with the old lion totem, heading west on an unfitted freight.When a locomotive was needed for the 1951 Festival of Britain, No 26020 was selected,and given stainless steel handrails and other embellishments. It also received special attention from the depot staff at reddish. A role in opening the new tunnel followed, and the resultant celebrity status meant it was also fitted with a train-heat boiler for passenger working. It all added up to a place in the national collection in York, where No 26020 stands today. *Peter Hughes / Colour-Rail DE1904*

Below: November 1969: Woodhead's passenger trains will be no more in seven weeks' time, and No 26049 *Jason*, looking distinctly old-fashioned in green, heads a rake of blue and grey Mk 1 coaches towards Manchester. The picture was taken at Bullhouse. *Les Nixon*

Right: Unfitted 16-ton coal wagons in the hands of Nos 76 033 and 76 038.

The latter engine swapped numbers with No 76 050 when it was fitted with multiple-unit equipment and air brakes in the mid-1970s — one of the second batch to be treated. Several locomotives changed numbers to create a block of MU-fitted and air-braked engines starting at 76 006 and ending at 76 039, with a few gaps for withdrawals. The locomotives outside this number range were left as unmodified, vacuum-only engines. *G. R. Jelly*

Above: Nos 76 014 and 76 006 roll down the gradient at Thurlstone, heading for Penistone, on the last day of the Woodhead line with the Trafford Park–Parkestone Quay Speedlink working in their care. The pair would later work back light to Barnsley Junction to take over the final MGR coal working later that evening. *Ken Braithwaite*

Right: No E26057 leaving Penistone with a Manchester-bound express in June 1969. *Ulysses* has just made it into full BR corporate blue livery and is hauling a full set of blue and grey coaches — a rarity, because no sooner had the blue colour scheme begun to make an impact than passenger services on the line ceased. *Gavin Morrison*

Above: A brace of '76s' grinds purposefully westwards with a haul of power-station coal in spring 1981, just a few weeks before closure. The leading locomotive, No 76 022, sports a broken multiple-unit jumper. The scene is Penistone Goods, by now disused. *Alan Whitehouse*

Right: Penistone Goods again, this time with a solo '76' heading a jumble of unfitted wagons east. By now the '76s' had lost even their works plates — they were generously provided with four apiece by Gorton. The patch of light paint on the cab side reveals where one of these was once fixed. *Ken Braithwaite*

Penistone station survived more or less untouched for several years after closure of the main line platforms — two others remained in use for Huddersfield–Sheffield trains. Even the platform canopies remained intact, as this view of Nos 76 025 and 76 030, heading for Wath Yard with MGR empties, shows. Electrification rules demanded a high contact wire at stations, level crossings and — in steam days — water columns. Normal height above rail level was 16ft; here, it is 20ft, giving the impression that the two locomotives are stretching to reach it. *John Denby*

After passenger services on the line finished, there was a steady stream of
charter trains. This example ran in the early 1970s. Pleasingly, it used a
single vacuum-only locomotive, No 76 049, formerly *Jason*, its name
reinstated for the day in chalk letters by a thoughtful enthusiast. It is seen
here at Penistone, heading west. *Alan Whitehouse*

Above: The electric passenger service had been running for only a few weeks when this picture of No 26005 was taken in August 1954. The locomotive is resplendent in red-lined black livery, and is trailing a set of coaches finished in the first corporate colour scheme of British Railways. Sadly, No 26005 was one of the first 'EM1s' to be scrapped, being taken out of service in 1970 after a working life of just 18 years. *J. B. McCann / Colour-Rail DE1643*

Right: The final 'EM1', No E26057, its *Ulysses* nameplate still in place, makes a fine sight as it rolls by Huddersfield Junction, heading west with a train of steelgirders in April 1970. The locomotive entered service in 1953 and lasted until February 1977, when falling traffic levels led to its withdrawal. *Peter Hughes / Colour-Rail DE547*

Left: Last of the line: the final coal train over Woodhead, a working to Fiddler's Ferry power station, near Warrington, is ready to leave Barnsley Junction, just to the east of Penistone, at about 10pm on Friday 17 July 1981. A small crowd had gathered to watch as Nos 76 014 and 76 006 arrived light and coupled onto the MGR set. A short pause, and it was all over. Coal was the overriding reason for the building of the Woodhead line. Now the final coal train had gone and the signalman at Barnsley Junction switched out the box for ever. A few hours later, in the early hours of Saturday, the last train of all passed over the line. *Alan Whitehouse*

Below: No E26056 *Triton*, wearing BR green, heads a rake of blue and grey stock interrupted by one maroon vehicle, near Thurgoland in December 1969. *Peter Hughes / Colour-Rail DE1909*

Below: No 76 029 running light between Thurgoland and Wortley on a spring morning in 1977. The '76s' were often repainted at Reddish depot, and some *ad hoc* colour schemes resulted, as with No 76 029's off-white pantographs. Other examples were finished with bright blue 'pans', and a handful of locomotives were turned out with their buffer-beams marked 'No 1 End' and 'No 2 End'. *Alan Whitehouse*

Right: Only a few weeks to go before the Woodhead's expresses get the chop, and No E26055 *Prometheus* runs into Deepcar station in November 1969 with a Sheffield-bound express. Shortly after the end of the passenger service, the 12 named locomotives (excluding *Tommy*) which had not already lost their nameplates had them removed to forestall freelance 'collecting'. *Peter Hughes / Colour-Rail DE1569*

Above: The weather has turned predictably nasty as a pair of air-braked '76s' head a freight through what was Deepcar station in mid-1975. Both these locomotives — whose numbers are unknown — were renumbered in BR's most economical style, with only two sets of numbers per locomotive. Others, for no obvious reason, carried four sets — one on each cab side — to the very end. *Alan Whitehouse*

Right: Deepcar was an important interchange point for traffic in and out of the steelworks. Scrap metal was one inbound commodity, being carried here in former 16-ton coal wagons in the charge of No 76 051 in September 1980. *Ken Braithwaite*

Left: A brace of air-fitted '76s' shunt at the head of the steelworks railway, which left the main line, descending in a steep horseshoe curve to the works on the valley floor. It was worked by the complex's own fleet of industrial diesels. The steelworks still provides traffic, and this portion of the Woodhead line has become a single-track branch. *Alan Whitehouse*

Above: No 76 022 in the Deepcar sidings — a view which shows clearly the 'lion' totem the locomotive carried until scrapping. *Alan Whitehouse*

Right: Driver's-eye view of No E26053 *Perseus* approaching with a Manchester express in August 1968. The train has just cleared the suburbs of Sheffield and is beginning the relentless climb to Penistone and then Dunford Bridge. *Gavin Morrison*

Left: The date is 1977 and No 76 025, together with No 76 030, coasts down the gradient through Neepsend on the outskirts of Sheffield with MGR empties for Rotherwood or Tinsley. The overhead line was extended into the new Tinsley Yard in 1965, but it never generated the expected traffic. *Les Nixon*

Above: The pioneer 'EM2', No 27000, wearing lined BR green, stands at Sheffield Victoria in September 1958. The locomotive was later named *Electra* and was to last just another 10 years with BR before being withdrawn and later sold to the Netherlands Railways. None of the 'EM2s' lasted long enough to carry Rail blue, or receive Class 77-series numbers. *G. Warnes / Colour-Rail DE535*

April 1966, and No E27003 *Diana* has just arrived at Victoria with an express from Manchester. Rain on the platforms and reflected light paint an evocative picture of a station long since swept away. *G. Warnes / Colour-Rail DE537*

No E27005 *Minerva* in BR green arrives in Platform 4 at Sheffield Victoria with what, according to the headcode on display, is a parcels train. The 'EM2s' were built for a mix of passenger and fitted freight work.
George M. Staddon / Colour-Rail DE1753

Left: In truth, the 'EM2s' were an unnecessary luxury. The 'EM1' fleet could handle any traffic that presented itself, given that the route over Woodhead had a line speed of 65mph. 'EM1' No E26055 *Prometheus* proves the point, as it waits to depart with an express service in 1968.
Gavin Morrison

Above: Victoria station survived for several years after closure in 1970: it was brought back to life for one glorious weekend in 1974 when Midland station was being resignalled. Shortly afterwards, demolition work began, and all that is left today is a single line to service Deepcar Steelworks. Much of the trackwork is still *in situ* as air-fitted '76s', 24 and 15, head a train of hoppers into the west end of the station in the early 1970s.
Alan Whitehouse

Left: The freight branch to Wombwell and Wath left the main Woodhead route at Barnsley Junction, immediately to the east of Penistone. About a mile along the line, MU-fitted Nos 76 013 and 76 026 approach Oxspring Tunnel with an empty MGR train for Wath Yard. One of the two bores is still in use for the single-track Barnsley–Penistone line. *G. R. Jelly*

Below: A 1966 view taken from West Silkstone Junction signalbox. Here the lines to Barnsley and Wath diverged. A westbound coal train is coming off the Worsborough branch; assisting in the rear will be another Class 76. A banking engine, which has arrived on an earlier train, is sitting in the bankers' siding. Regenerative braking meant that banking engines could also assist loose-coupled trains on the downhill run from West Silkstone to Wombwell. Both engines would shift into regenerative mode when the train was on the move, avoiding the need to pin down wagon brakes for the descent. *Peter Howard*

Right: Moving on 10 years, some locomotives have been modified to operate in pairs and with air braking. Neither feature would be necessary for this train: the wagons are still the same loose-coupled 16-tonners and a banker would still be required behind the brake van for safety reasons. But, as the Class 76 fleet was thinned out, a pair of modified locomotives (rather than a single vacuum-only example) was often all that was available. *Alan Whitehouse*

Left: August 1980, and No 76 054 has just arrived at West Silkstone Junction having banked a loose-coupled train up the Wentworth Incline. The locomotive is pausing while the crew change ends before rolling back down to Wombwell Main Exchange sidings, and looks the picture of dejection: nameplate long since removed, and even the works plates now gone. The paintwork is chipped and fading, and it is obvious that the end is not far away. *Alan Whitehouse*

Below: Despite No 76 054's condition, its crew still have an obvious pride in their charge. Banking engines always carried two crew and on this day it was driver Walter Carroll and secondman Peter Goode. *Alan Whitehouse*

No 76 053 heads the 8M17 Monckton–Northwich coke train out of Silkstone No 2 Tunnel in September 1980. The two Silkstone tunnels were only around 200yd apart, on a curving steep incline. In steam days, the crews of four locomotives — two train engines and two bankers — would be taking a brief, welcome breath of fresh air before plunging into No 1 Tunnel. In contrast, electric traction made light work. *Ken Braithwaite*

Right: A westbound train of steel passes Wentworth Junction's starter on a May Saturday morning in 1966. The 'EM1' is displaying the headcode for a through freight train, indicating it will not stop again until a change of traction, probably at Mottram Yard. *Peter Howard*

Below: Wentworth Junction, and No E26040 heads an eastbound freight towards Wath in the summer of 1971. It was unusual to see a single-headed train going down the incline, and the explanation for the locomotive's solo feat is that this is a fitted train, with ample braking power. *Alan Whitehouse*

Ten years later, and Wentworth Junction box is a derelict shell, the colliery it served long closed. An unidentified pair of MU-fitted '76s' head west. By this time traffic was becoming sparse, and it was common for crews to work back home light-engine because there was no work for them to do.
Alan Whitehouse

Right: Last hours of the Worsborough branch: Nos 76 012 and 76 007 bank the final MGR coal working over the branch on the morning of 17 July 1981. The ensemble — two train locomotives, a set of 30 MGR wagons and the bankers — has just cleared Kendall Green crossing. MGR trains from Wath Yard to Fiddler's Ferry Power Station had been the branch's staple traffic for several years. *Ken Braithwaite*

KENDALL GREEN CROSSING

Left: It is shortly after midday and Class 76s Nos 76 006 and 76 014 approach Kendall Green crossing with the final working over the Worsborough branch. Within hours the signalboxes had been stripped of their block instruments and the crossing gates padlocked, the branch closed forever. *Alan Whitehouse*

Below: The crossing gates are closed for the final time. The gates here were always manually operated, with no remote gatewheel despite the high levels of traffic in the line's heyday. Many boxes along the Worsborough branch were almost working museums — most still had a complete set of Great Central Railway block instruments and bells, 58 years after Grouping and 29 years after electrification!
Alan Whitehouse

Below and right: The Worsborough branch was built purely as a freight route when constantly rising volumes of coal threatened to swamp the system. Passenger trains were a rarity, but for many years the local Barrow Working Men's Club at Worsborough used the branch for its annual outing. A procession of excursion trains would load their passengers using nothing more sophisticated than sets of crude wooden steps set up in a former goods yard between Worsborough Bridge and Glasshouse level crossings. In these two 1967 pictures, train 1F79 loads passengers who are milling around on the down line, while, a little later, train 1F78 powers away over Glasshouse crossing heading for Cleethorpes. The manœuvre was repeated at the end of the day, often in darkness — a health and safety nightmare, at least by today's standards. *Peter Howard*

Below: It was not just the exposed Pennine section of the Manchester–Sheffield–Wath system that suffered from extreme weather. This is Glasshouse crossing, and an unidentified vacuum-only '76' banks the Monckton–Northwich coke working westwards in the teeth of a blizzard. The coke train was one of the final single-engine turns over the branch. As trains became heavier and more wagons were air-braked, pairs of MU-fitted locos became more and more common. *Adrian Gilmartin*

Right: A pair of multiple-unit-fitted Class 76s bring up the rear of a loaded steel train as it grinds up the incline at Lewden crossing. A corner of the rear cab of the leading pair of locomotives can be glimpsed through the trees. The modified '76s' were all fitted with the 'Clear Call' telephone system, which routed conversations between trains and banker drivers via the overhead power line. MGR coal trains were about a quarter of a mile long, so some form of communication was essential for safe working. *Ken Braithwaite*

Below: Class 76 No76 030 heads a load of unbraked 16-ton coal wagons near Lewden crossing, the first of five level crossings in the space of less than two miles. The picture was taken in the summer of 1980, and this working to Garston Docks, Liverpool, was the last regular loose-coupled coal train on the branch, all other traffic by now being conveyed in block MGR trains. It would normally be headed by a vacuum-only locomotive and banked by a second '76', but by now there were only a handful of unmodified '76s' left in service and multiple-unit pairs were often split to work as singles. *Alan Whitehouse*

Right: Wombwell Main sidings were a busy place almost to the end. Here the pioneer 'EM1', No 26000 *Tommy*, adds to the workload as it pilots an enthusiasts' special headed by 'B1' No 61360 in June 1964.
C. R. Gordon Stuart / Colour-Rail DE1808

Left: By now British Rail's oldest operational locomotive, No 76 001 stands at Wombwell Main sidings whilst on banking duty in the autumn of 1980. Note the damaged axlebox; many small defects on the class were now going unrepaired in anticipation of closure. *Alan Whitehouse*

Above: Sixteen years earlier, in 1964, 'EM1' No 26025 stands in almost the same spot, quite probably performing the same banking duties. Unusually, the loco is in green livery, but with the early 'cycling lion' totem. *Peter Howard*

Below: A pair of MU-fitted locomotives with a loaded coke train approaching Aldham Junction on the first leg of their trip across the Pennines in 1978. Aldham Junction was where the main line from Barnsley rejoined the Worsborough branch, and from there to Wath Yard was once quadruple track. Those days are long gone, but a set of redundant rails can be seen in the foreground. *Alan Whitehouse*

Right: Class 76s performed little trip work; most colliery and works sidings were not electrified, so a picture of one running 'engine and brake' is a comparatively rare sight. This is No E26057 near Elsecar Junction in June 1970. *Ken Braithwaite*

Left: Classic Worsborough branch working in the 1970s. A pair of air-braked '76s', Nos 76 038 and 76 035, leave Wath Yard with a westbound haul of coal in a block train of 30 MGR wagons in June 1978. The locomotives were part of the second batch to be converted; the vacuum-brake hoses have been removed — a reflection of the decline in vacuum-braked stock. The train would run with the two train engines to Wombwell Main sidings, where another pair of '76s' would couple on at the rear and bank it the eight miles or so to West Silkstone Junction.
Ken Braithwaite

Above and right: Two views of the shed at Wath. The first, dating from 1957, depicts a comparatively rare appearance by a Class EM2 at Wath. The 'EM2s' spent almost all their time on the Sheffield–Manchester expresses, with other turns on fast fitted freights, so a trip down the Worsborough branch was uncommon. A corner of the new shed built to house the electric fleet is also visible. In later years the overhead line equipment was removed, confining the '76s' to the shed yard, as seen in this 1980 shot of 76 011 and 76 029.
RCT / Colour-Rail DE1302;
Alan Whitehouse